Plant and Grow

CONTENTS

Help with Work   page 4

A Yam in a Cup   page 14

NATIONAL GEOGRAPHIC

School Publishing

Hampton-Brown

Sounds for y, qu, x, k

Look at each picture. Read the words.

Example:

yak

quack

fo**x**

king

High Frequency **Words**

| for |
| grow |
| keep |
| look |
| or |
| when |

Key Words

Look at the pictures.
Read the sentences.

ox

yam

Help!

1. We like to **grow** yams.
2. **When** we work, we **look** **for** help.
3. We **keep** an ox and a yak.
4. The ox **or** the yak can help us.

What do they grow?

Phonics Games
NGReach.com

3

Help with Work

by Lada Kratky

illustrated by Durga Bernhard

It is a lot of work to grow plants.

Look at that man with his yak.

That man's yak helps him with his work.

Look at Quin with his ox.

Quin's ox helps him with his work, too.

Look at Kim with his pup.

Can Kim's pup help him with his work? ❖

Sounds for y, qu, x, k

Read these words.

yak	Quin	Ken	fox
ox	yam	quit	kit

Find the words that start with **y**.
Then find words with **qu**, **x** and **k**.
Use letters to build them.

Talk Together

Choose words from
the box to talk about
what you see in the picture.

Ox can help.

Fox can not help.

Ken

Quin

u

Words with Short u

Look at the pictures. Read the words.

Example:

s**u**n

m**u**g

c**u**p

b**u**g

j**u**g

b**u**d

High Frequency Words

for

grow

keep

look

or

when

Key Words

Read each sentence. Look at the pictures.

Grow a Yam

1. **When** you **grow** a yam, do what I do.
2. Put it in a cup **or** a mug.
3. **Keep** it wet.
4. **Look for** bugs.
5. Have fun!

How do you grow a yam?

GO! **Phonics Games**
🡒 NGReach.com

A Yam in a Cup

by Lada Kratky
illustrated by Vanessa Newton

This is a yam.

cup

Put the yam in a cup or a mug.

Keep the yam very wet in the cup.

Keep the yam in the sun.

bud

The yam has a bug on a bud!

Do not cut that bud!

When I grow yams in cups, it is for the
fun of it! What can you grow in a cup? ❖

Words with Short **u**

Read these words.

yam	cut	mug	pet
cup	bug	jug	fun

Find the words with short **u**.
Use letters to build them.

Talk **Together**

Choose words from the box
above to tell your partner what is wet.

The _yam_
is wet.

Yams for the Yaks!

Look for 10 yams for the yaks. Take turns telling your partner where the yams are.

Acknowledgments
Grateful acknowledgment is given to the authors, artists, photographers, museums, publishers, and agents for permission to reprint copyrighted material. Every effort has been made to secure the appropriate permission. If any omissions have been made or if corrections are required, please contact the Publisher.

Photographic Credits
CVR (Cover) UpperCut Images/Alamy Images. **2** (bl) Digital Vision/Getty Images. (br) Massimo Borchi/Atlantide Phototravel/Corbis. (tl) Grigory Kubatyan/Shutterstock. (tr) Craig Dingle/Shutterstock. **3** (b) Liz Garza Williams/Hampton-Brown/National Geographic School Publishing. (l) brytta/iStockphoto. (r) Sharon Day/Shutterstock. **11** (l) Liz Garza Williams/Hampton-Brown/National Geographic School Publishing. (r) Liz Garza Williams/Hampton-Brown/National Geographic School Publishing. **12** (bl) Danny Smythe/Shutterstock. (br) PhotoDisc/Getty Images. (cl) MonicaJohansen/Shutterstock. (cr) pixelman/Shutterstock. (tl) Creatas/Jupiterimages. (tr) Stockbyte/Getty Images. **13** (b) Liz Garza Williams/Hampton-Brown/National Geographic School Publishing. **21** (t) Liz Garza Williams/Hampton-Brown/National Geographic School Publishing. **23** (b) Liz Garza Williams/Hampton-Brown/National Geographic School Publishing.

Illustrator Credits
4-10 Durga Bernhard; **11, 13, 21, 22-23** Jim Paillot; **14-20** Vanessa Newton

The National Geographic Society
John M. Fahey, Jr., President & Chief Executive Officer
Gilbert M. Grosvenor, Chairman of the Board

National Geographic School Publishing
Hampton-Brown
www.NGSP.com

Printed in the USA.
LSC Communications, Menasha, WI

ISBN:978-0-7362-8026-6

16 17 18 19
10 9 8 7 6